100 facts
T REX

100 facts
T REX

Steve Parker

Consultant: Rupert Matthews

Miles
Kelly

First published in 2009 by Miles Kelly Publishing Ltd
Harding's Barn, Bardfield End Green, Thaxted, Essex, CM6 3PX

This edition printed 2012

4 6 8 10 9 7 5

Publishing Director: Belinda Gallagher
Creative Director: Jo Cowan
Image Manager: Lorraine King
Indexer: Jane Parker
Production Manager: Elizabeth Collins
Reprographics: Stephan Davis, Jennifer Hunt, Ian Paulyn, Thom Allaway
Reprographics Assistant: Charlie Pearson
Assets: Lorraine King

ISBN 978-1-84810-171-5

Printed in China

British Library Cataloguing-in-Publication Data
A catalogue record for this book is available from the British Library

ACKNOWLEDGEMENTS
The publishers would like to thank the following artists
who have contributed to this book:

Mike Foster, Ian Jackson Mike Saunders
Cover artwork: Ian Jackson

All other artworks from the Miles Kelly Artwork Bank

The publishers would like to thank the following sources
for the use of their photographs:

Page 6 Photos 12/Alamy; 16(t) Robert Clark/Photolibrary, 16(b) Corbis; 26 Salvatore Vasapolli/Photolibrary;
32 Bettman/Corbis; 33 Bettman/Corbis; 35 Layne Kennedy/Corbis; 36 DK Limited/Corbis;
37 Volker Steger/Science Photo Library; 38 Reuters/Ho Old; 39 Steve Vider/Photolibrary; 40 Louie Psihoyos/Corbis;
41 Jane: Courtesy of Burpee Museum of Natural History; 42 Louie Psihoyos/Corbis; 44 © 20thC.Fox/Everett/Rex Features;
45(t) Handout/Getty Images; 45(b) Topham Picture Point/Topfoto; 46 Nils Jorgensen/Rex Features

All other photographs are from:

Corel, digitalSTOCK, digitalvision, Fotolia.com, iStockphoto.com, John Foxx,
PhotoAlto, PhotoDisc, PhotoEssentials, PhotoPro, Stockbyte

Made with paper from a sustainable forest

www.mileskelly.net
info@mileskelly.net

www.factsforprojects.com

Contents

Long live the king!

1 Almost everyone has heard of *Tyrannosaurus rex*. Wasn't it the biggest dinosaur of all time, the greatest meat eater with a mouth big enough to swallow a car and teeth as long as swords? Not one of these 'facts' is true. Certainly *Tyrannosaurus rex* is one of the world's most famous animals. Even though it died out 65 million years ago, it 'lives on' in movies, toys and games, as statues and works of art, and in music and songs. However, *Tyrannosaurus rex* is also the subject of many mistaken beliefs.

▶ A scene from the 2005 movie *King Kong*. With a mighty roar *Tyrannosaurus rex* bares its huge mouth filled with sharp teeth and prepares to attack. Images like this are familiar — but are they correct? For example, did *T rex* really roar loudly?

Terror of its age

▲ The last dinosaurs of the Late Cretaceous Period ranged from small, speedy hunters such as *Avimimus* to giant plant eaters, three-horned *Triceratops*, spiky *Edmontonia*, hadrosaurs or 'duckbilled' dinosaurs with strange head crests, and of course *T rex*.

KEY

1 *Tyrannosaurus rex*	5 *Parasaurolophus*	9 *Struthiomimus*
2 *Triceratops*	6 *Lambeosaurus*	10 *Albertosaurus*
3 *Stegoceras*	7 *Avimimus*	11 *Therizinosaurus*
4 *Edmontonia*	8 *Corythosaurus*	12 *Euoplocephalus*

2 *T rex*'s full name is *Tyrannosaurus rex*, which means 'king of the tyrant lizards'. However, it wasn't a lizard. It was a large carnivorous or meat-eating animal in the reptile group known as the dinosaurs.

3 Dinosaurs, or 'terrible lizards', lived during a time called the Mesozoic Era (251–65 million years ago). The first dinosaurs appeared about 230 million years ago and all had died out, or become extinct, by 65 million years ago.

4 There were hundreds of kinds of dinosaurs. *Plateosaurus* was a bus-sized herbivore (plant eater) from 210 million years ago. *Brachiosaurus* was a giant herbivore from 150 million years ago. *Deinonychus* was a fierce hunter from about 110 million years ago, and was about the size of an adult human.

QUIZ

Which of these extinct animals were dinosaurs?

Pterodactyl
Tyrannosaurus rex
Woolly mammoth
Archaeopteryx   Triceratops
Plateosaurus   Ammonite

Answer:
Tyrannosaurus rex,
Triceratops, Plateosaurus

5 *Tyrannosaurus rex* lived well after all of these dinosaurs. Its time was the last part of the Mesozoic Era, known as the Cretaceous Period (145–65 million years ago), from about 68 to 65 million years ago. *T rex* was one of the very last dinosaurs.

ERA	PERIOD	MYA (Million years ago)
		— 70
		— 80
		— 90
	CRETACEOUS 145–65 MYA	— 100
		— 110
		— 120
		— 130
MESOZOIC		— 140
		— 150
		— 160
	JURASSIC 200–145 MYA	— 170
		— 180
		— 190
		— 200
		— 210
	TRIASSIC 251–200 MYA	— 220
		— 230
		— 240
		— 250

Jurassic Period: *Allosaurus* was a big meat-eating dinosaur

Triassic Period: *Herrerasaurus* was one of the first dinosaurs

◄ Dinosaurs ruled the land for 160 million years — longer than any other animal group.

9

A giant predator

6 The size of big, fierce animals such as great white sharks, tigers and crocodiles can be exaggerated (made bigger). People often think *T rex* was bigger than it really was.

7 A full-grown *T rex* was over 12 metres long and more than 3 metres high at the hips. It could rear up and raise its head to more than 5 metres above the ground.

Brachiosaurus
13 metres tall
25 metres nose to tail
40-plus tonnes in weight

8 *Tyrannosaurus rex* was not such a giant compared to some plant-eating animals. It was about the same weight as today's African bush elephant, half the size of the extinct imperial mammoth, and one-tenth as heavy as some of the biggest plant-eating dinosaurs.

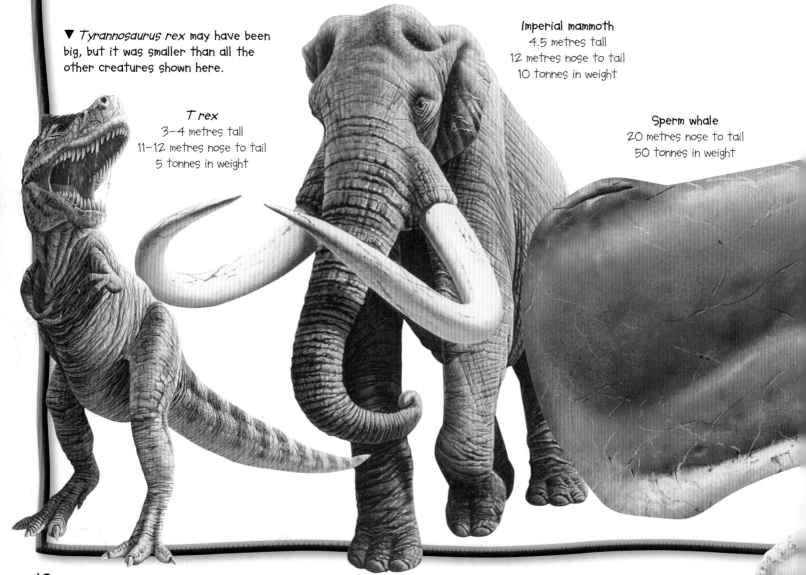

▼ *Tyrannosaurus rex* may have been big, but it was smaller than all the other creatures shown here.

Imperial mammoth
4.5 metres tall
12 metres nose to tail
10 tonnes in weight

T rex
3–4 metres tall
11–12 metres nose to tail
5 tonnes in weight

Sperm whale
20 metres nose to tail
50 tonnes in weight

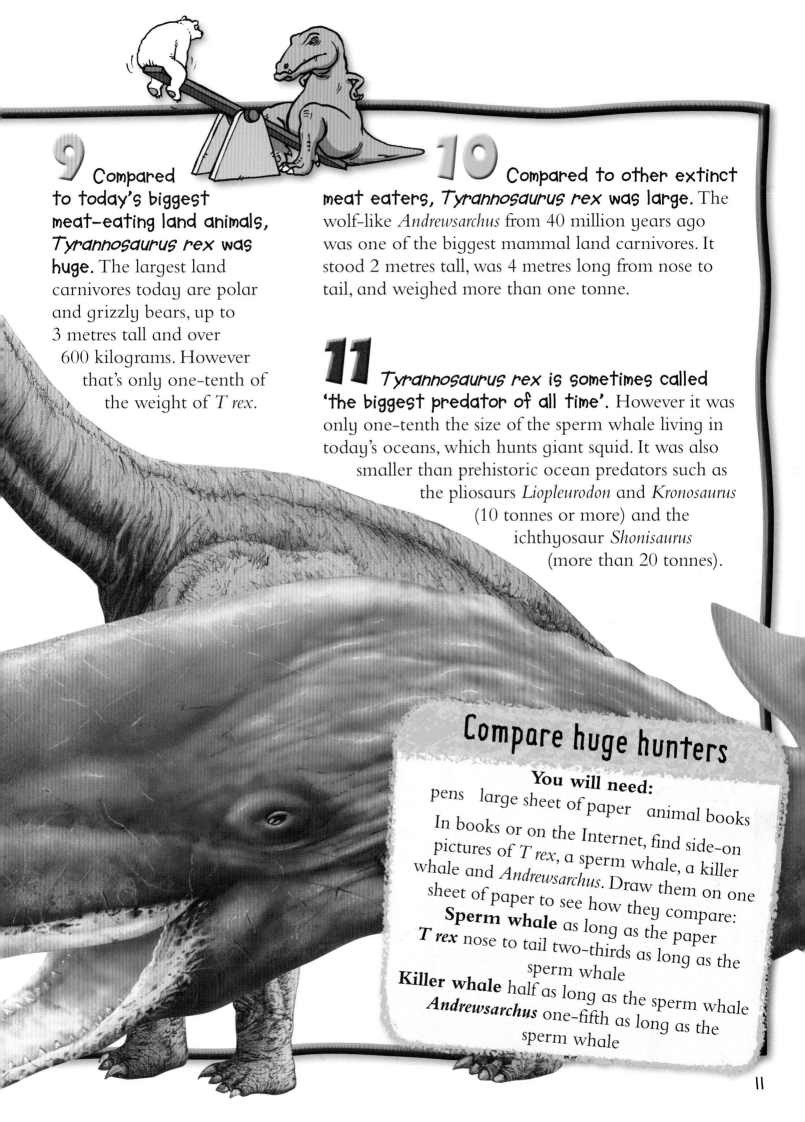

9 Compared to today's biggest meat-eating land animals, *Tyrannosaurus rex* was huge. The largest land carnivores today are polar and grizzly bears, up to 3 metres tall and over 600 kilograms. However that's only one-tenth of the weight of *T rex*.

10 Compared to other extinct meat eaters, *Tyrannosaurus rex* was large. The wolf-like *Andrewsarchus* from 40 million years ago was one of the biggest mammal land carnivores. It stood 2 metres tall, was 4 metres long from nose to tail, and weighed more than one tonne.

11 *Tyrannosaurus rex* is sometimes called 'the biggest predator of all time'. However it was only one-tenth the size of the sperm whale living in today's oceans, which hunts giant squid. It was also smaller than prehistoric ocean predators such as the pliosaurs *Liopleurodon* and *Kronosaurus* (10 tonnes or more) and the ichthyosaur *Shonisaurus* (more than 20 tonnes).

Compare huge hunters

You will need:
pens   large sheet of paper   animal books

In books or on the Internet, find side-on pictures of *T rex*, a sperm whale, a killer whale and *Andrewsarchus*. Draw them on one sheet of paper to see how they compare:
Sperm whale as long as the paper
T rex nose to tail two-thirds as long as the sperm whale
Killer whale half as long as the sperm whale
Andrewsarchus one-fifth as long as the sperm whale

Profile of T rex

12 Fossil experts can work out what an extinct animal such a *Tyrannosaurus rex* looked like when it was alive. They study the size, shape, length, thickness and other details of its fossil bones, teeth, claws and other parts.

13 The tail of *T rex* was almost half its total length. It had a wide, muscular base and was thick and strong almost to the tip, quite unlike the long, thin, whip-like tails of other dinosaurs such as *Diplodocus*.

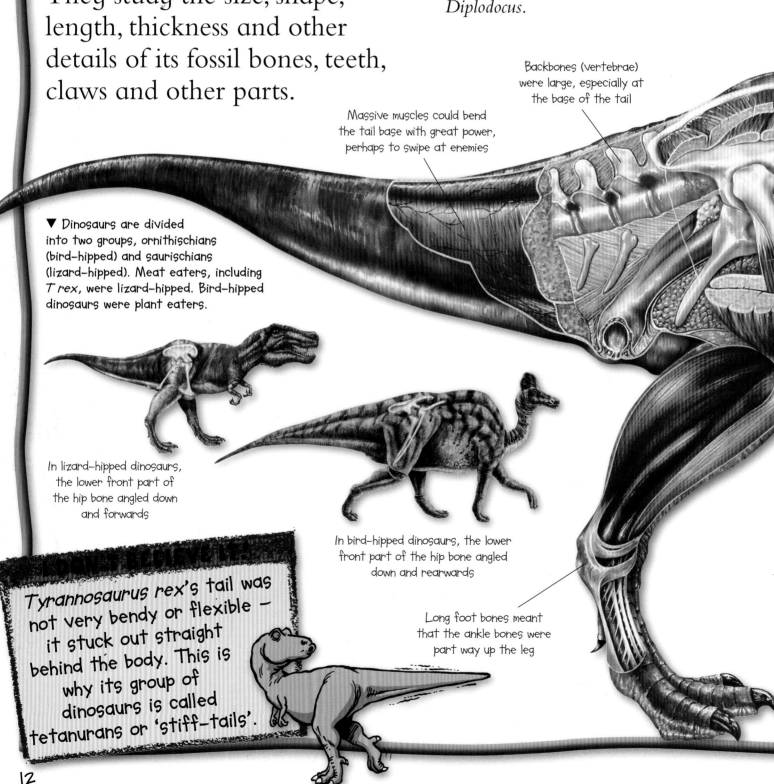

Backbones (vertebrae) were large, especially at the base of the tail

Massive muscles could bend the tail base with great power, perhaps to swipe at enemies

▼ Dinosaurs are divided into two groups, ornithischians (bird-hipped) and saurischians (lizard-hipped). Meat eaters, including *T rex*, were lizard-hipped. Bird-hipped dinosaurs were plant eaters.

In lizard-hipped dinosaurs, the lower front part of the hip bone angled down and forwards

In bird-hipped dinosaurs, the lower front part of the hip bone angled down and rearwards

Long foot bones meant that the ankle bones were part way up the leg

I DON'T BELIEVE IT!

Tyrannosaurus rex's tail was not very bendy or flexible – it stuck out straight behind the body. This is why its group of dinosaurs is called tetanurans or 'stiff-tails'.

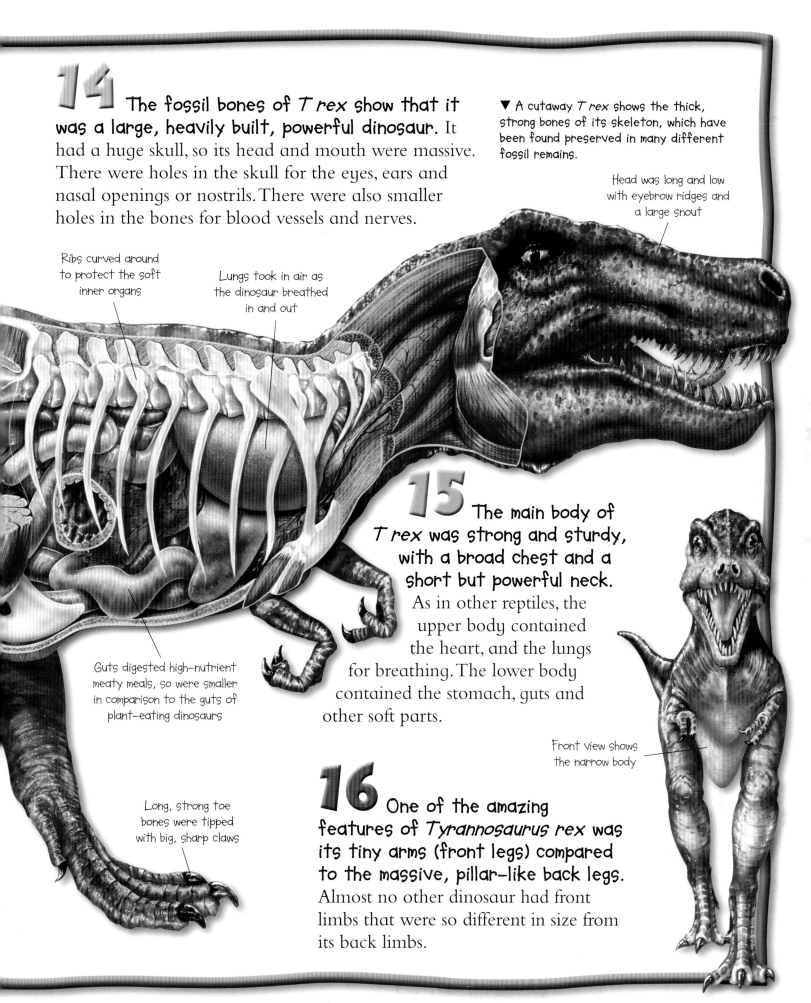

14 The fossil bones of *T rex* show that it was a large, heavily built, powerful dinosaur. It had a huge skull, so its head and mouth were massive. There were holes in the skull for the eyes, ears and nasal openings or nostrils. There were also smaller holes in the bones for blood vessels and nerves.

▼ A cutaway *T rex* shows the thick, strong bones of its skeleton, which have been found preserved in many different fossil remains.

Head was long and low with eyebrow ridges and a large snout

Ribs curved around to protect the soft inner organs

Lungs took in air as the dinosaur breathed in and out

15 The main body of *T rex* was strong and sturdy, with a broad chest and a short but powerful neck. As in other reptiles, the upper body contained the heart, and the lungs for breathing. The lower body contained the stomach, guts and other soft parts.

Guts digested high-nutrient meaty meals, so were smaller in comparison to the guts of plant-eating dinosaurs

Front view shows the narrow body

Long, strong toe bones were tipped with big, sharp claws

16 One of the amazing features of *Tyrannosaurus rex* was its tiny arms (front legs) compared to the massive, pillar-like back legs. Almost no other dinosaur had front limbs that were so different in size from its back limbs.

Was T rex clever?

▼ Many dinosaurs had eyes on the sides of the head, giving good all-round vision but not a detailed front view. T rex had forward-facing eyes.

View from forward-facing eyes

View from sideways-facing eyes

► T rex probably used its long tongue to lick and taste meat before it started to eat.

17 **The skull of T rex is well known from several good fossils.** They show that the large eyes were set at an angle so they looked forwards rather than to the sides. This allowed T rex to see an object in front with both eyes and judge its distance well.

18 **As far as we know dinosaurs, like other reptiles, lacked ear flaps.** Instead they had eardrums of thin skin on the sides of their heads so they could hear.

Brain

Nasal openings
(nares)

▲ The braincase of *T rex* was small compared to the size of the whole skull. Nerves connected the brain to the eyes, nose, ears and other body parts.

19 *T rex*'s big nasal openings were at the top of its snout. They opened into a very large chamber inside the skull, which detected smells floating in the air. *T rex*'s sense of smell, like its eyesight, was very good.

20 Some fossils even show the size and shape of *T rex*'s brain! The brain was in a casing called the cranium in the upper rear of the skull. This can be seen in well-preserved skulls. The space inside shows the brain's shape.

I DON'T BELIEVE IT!
The eyeballs of *Tyrannosaurus rex* were up to 8 centimetres across – but those of today's giant squid are almost 30 centimetres!

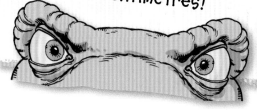

21 *Tyrannosaurus rex* had the biggest brain of almost any dinosaur. The parts dealing with the sense of smell, called the olfactory lobes, were especially large. So *T rex* had keen senses of sight, hearing and especially smell. And it wasn't stupid.

What big teeth!

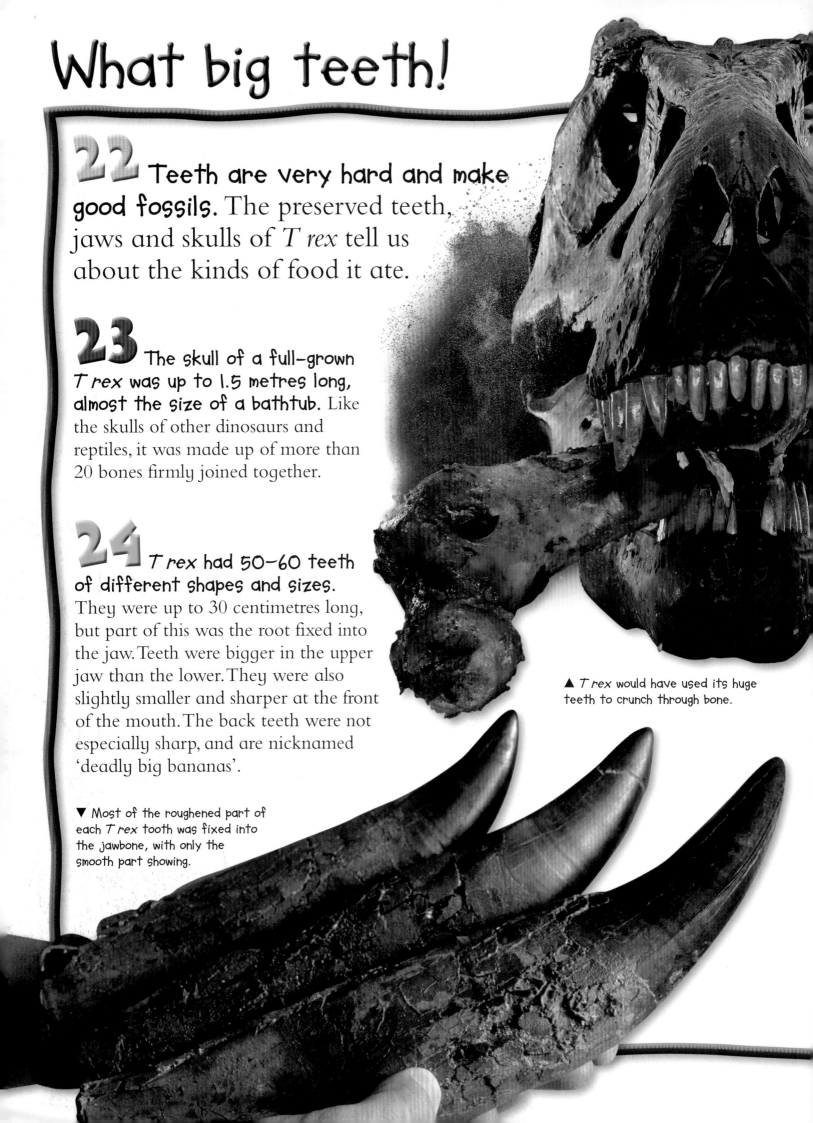

22 **Teeth are very hard and make good fossils.** The preserved teeth, jaws and skulls of *T rex* tell us about the kinds of food it ate.

23 **The skull of a full-grown *T rex* was up to 1.5 metres long, almost the size of a bathtub.** Like the skulls of other dinosaurs and reptiles, it was made up of more than 20 bones firmly joined together.

24 *T rex* had 50–60 teeth of different shapes and sizes. They were up to 30 centimetres long, but part of this was the root fixed into the jaw. Teeth were bigger in the upper jaw than the lower. They were also slightly smaller and sharper at the front of the mouth. The back teeth were not especially sharp, and are nicknamed 'deadly big bananas'.

▼ Most of the roughened part of each *T rex* tooth was fixed into the jawbone, with only the smooth part showing.

▲ *T rex* would have used its huge teeth to crunch through bone.

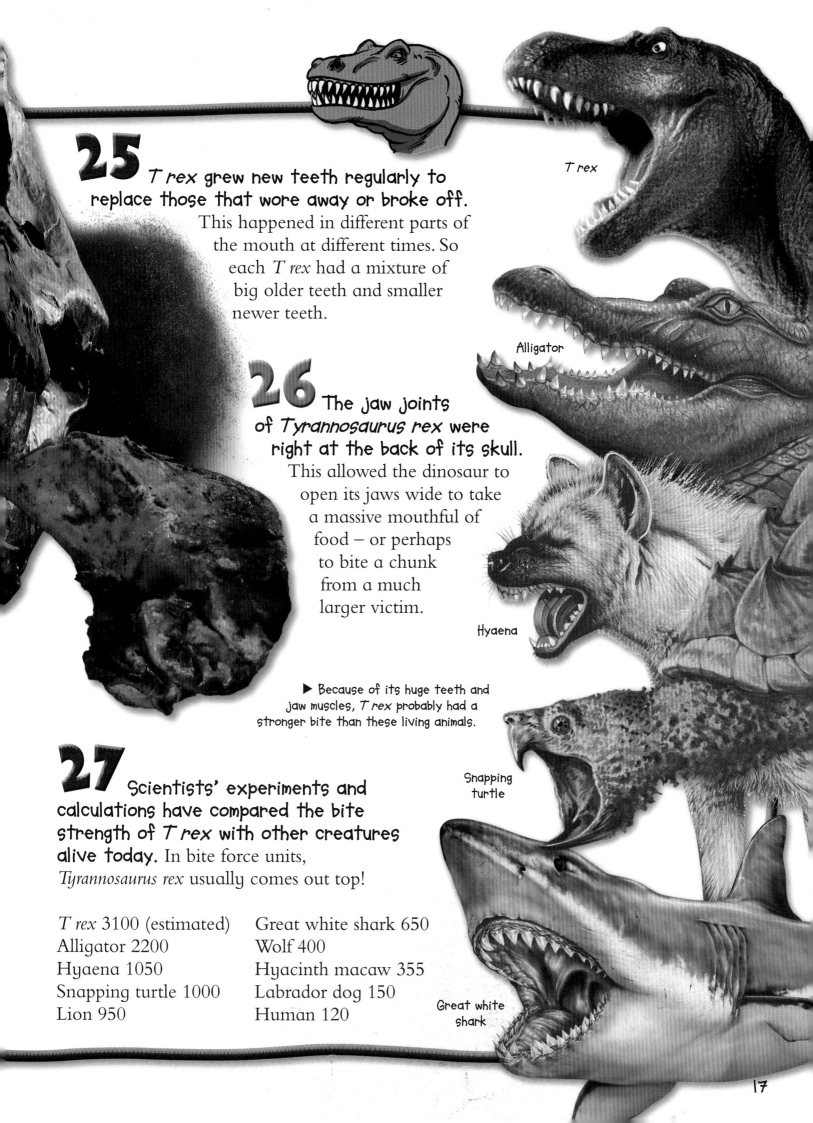

25 *T rex* grew new teeth regularly to replace those that wore away or broke off. This happened in different parts of the mouth at different times. So each *T rex* had a mixture of big older teeth and smaller newer teeth.

T rex

26 The jaw joints of *Tyrannosaurus rex* were right at the back of its skull. This allowed the dinosaur to open its jaws wide to take a massive mouthful of food – or perhaps to bite a chunk from a much larger victim.

Alligator

Hyaena

▶ Because of its huge teeth and jaw muscles, *T rex* probably had a stronger bite than these living animals.

Snapping turtle

27 Scientists' experiments and calculations have compared the bite strength of *T rex* with other creatures alive today. In bite force units, *Tyrannosaurus rex* usually comes out top!

T rex 3100 (estimated)
Alligator 2200
Hyaena 1050
Snapping turtle 1000
Lion 950

Great white shark 650
Wolf 400
Hyacinth macaw 355
Labrador dog 150
Human 120

Great white shark

Tiny arms, big legs

28 *Tyrannosaurus rex's strangest features were its tiny arms.* In fact, they were about the same size as the arms of an adult human, even though *T rex* was more than 50 times bigger than a person. Yet the arms were not weak. They had powerful muscles and two strong clawed fingers.

▶ *T rex's* arms were so small, they could not even be used for passing food to the mouth.

29 *What did Tyrannosaurus rex use its mini-arms for?* There have been many suggestions such as holding onto a victim while biting, pushing itself off the ground if it fell over, and holding onto a partner at breeding time. Perhaps we will never know the true reason.

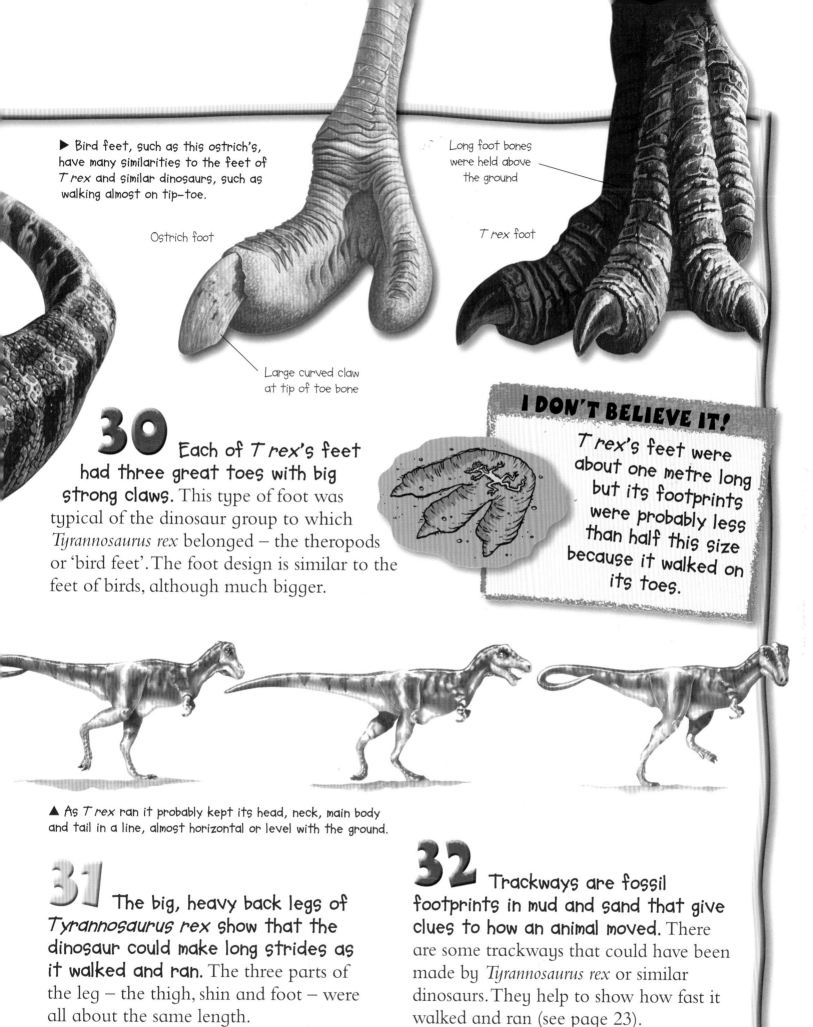

► Bird feet, such as this ostrich's, have many similarities to the feet of *T rex* and similar dinosaurs, such as walking almost on tip-toe.

Ostrich foot

Long foot bones were held above the ground

T rex foot

Large curved claw at tip of toe bone

30
Each of *T rex*'s feet had three great toes with big strong claws. This type of foot was typical of the dinosaur group to which *Tyrannosaurus rex* belonged – the theropods or 'bird feet'. The foot design is similar to the feet of birds, although much bigger.

I DON'T BELIEVE IT!
T rex's feet were about one metre long but its footprints were probably less than half this size because it walked on its toes.

▲ As *T rex* ran it probably kept its head, neck, main body and tail in a line, almost horizontal or level with the ground.

31
The big, heavy back legs of *Tyrannosaurus rex* show that the dinosaur could make long strides as it walked and ran. The three parts of the leg – the thigh, shin and foot – were all about the same length.

32
Trackways are fossil footprints in mud and sand that give clues to how an animal moved. There are some trackways that could have been made by *Tyrannosaurus rex* or similar dinosaurs. They help to show how fast it walked and ran (see page 23).

What did T rex eat?

33 Tyrannosaurus rex was a huge hunter, so it probably ate big prey. Other large dinosaurs of its time and place were plant eaters. They included three-horned *Triceratops* and its cousins, and various 'duckbilled' dinosaurs (hadrosaurs) such as *Parasaurolophus* and *Edmontosaurus*.

▼ The giant pterosaur (flying reptile) *Quetzalcoatlus* lived at about the same time as *T rex*. It may have pecked at the remains of a *T rex* kill after the dinosaur had finished feasting.

34 T rex could have used its huge mouth, strong teeth and powerful jaw muscles to attack these big plant eaters. It may have lunged at a victim with one massive bite to cause a slashing wound. Then it would retreat a short distance and wait for the prey to weaken from blood loss before moving in to feed.

◄ An adult *Triceratops* would be a fierce foe for *T rex* to tackle. However young, sick and old *Triceratops* might have been easier to kill.

35 One fossil of *Triceratops* has scratch-like gouge marks on its large, bony neck frill. These could have been made by *Tyrannosaurus rex* teeth. The marks are about the correct distance apart, matching the spacing of *T rex* teeth.

► The hadrosaur *Parasaurolophus* might have made loud trumpeting noises through its hollow tube-like head crest, to warn others in its herd that *T rex* was near.

A coprolite found in 1995 in Saskatchewan, Canada was probably produced by *T rex*. It was 42 centimetres long, 15 centimetres wide and 12 centimetres high!

► Coprolites can be broken apart or sawn through to study the bits of bones, teeth and other items inside.

36 Coprolites are preserved lumps of animal dung or droppings, fossilized into hard stone. Several large coprolites have been found that could be from *Tyrannosaurus rex*. They show many jumbled fragments of bone from its victims, including young *Edmontosaurus* and *Triceratops*.

37 In some dinosaurs, several fossil skeletons have been found preserved together, suggesting they lived as a pack or herd. The remains of several *Tyrannosaurus rex* have also been found in this way, which might suggest a family or a pack-hunting group. Some experts say that more evidence is needed for this idea.

► Armoured dinosaurs like *Euoplocephalus* may have defended themselves against *T rex* by swinging their heavy, clubbed tails.

Hunter or scavenger?

38 Was *T rex* an active hunter that chased after its victims? Was it an ambush predator that hid in wait to rush out at prey? Was it a scavenger that ate any dead or dying dinosaurs it found? Or did it chase other dinosaurs from their kills and steal the meal for itself?

39 To be an active pursuit hunter, *T rex* must have been able to run fast. Scientists have tried to work out its running speed using models and computers, and by comparisons with other animals.

Who does what?

Research these animals living today and find out if they are mainly fast hunters, sneaky ambushers or scavengers.
Tiger Cheetah Hyaena
Crocodile Vulture
African wild dog

▶ *Tyrannosaurus rex* may have run down smaller dinosaurs such as these *Prenocephale*, perhaps rushing out from its hiding place in a clump of trees.

▲ When scavenging, *T rex* might sniff out a dinosaur that had died from illness or injury.

▲ When hunting, *T rex* would be at risk from injury, such as from the horns of *Triceratops*.

40 Some estimates for the running speed of *T rex* are as fast as 50 kilometres an hour, others as slow as 15 kilometres an hour. Most give a speed of between 20 and 30 kilometres an hour. This is slightly slower than a human sprinter, but probably faster than typical *T rex* prey such as *Triceratops*.

42 Several *T rex* fossils show injuries to body parts such as shins, ribs, neck and jaws. These could have been made by victims fighting back, suggesting that *T rex* hunted live prey.

▶ *T rex* would tear and rip flesh from large prey, gulp in lumps and swallow them whole.

41 Evidence that *T rex* was a scavenger includes its very well developed sense of smell for sniffing out dead, rotting bodies. Also, its powerful teeth could not chew food repeatedly like we do, but they could crush bones at first bite to get at the nutritious jelly-like marrow inside. Maybe a hungry *Tyrannosaurus rex* simply ate anything it could catch or find, so it was a hunter, ambusher and scavenger all in one.

Growing up

43 Did *T rex* live in groups? Most of its fossils are of lone individuals. Some were found near other specimens of *T rex*. These could have been preserved near each other by chance, or they could have been a group that all died together.

Embryo   Yolk

▲ A baby dinosaur developed as an embryo in its egg, fed by nutrients from the yolk.

▶ The baby probably hatched out by biting through the tough shell, which was flexible like leather.

44 Living reptiles lay eggs that hatch into young, and dinosaurs such as *T rex* probably did the same. Many fossil dinosaur eggs have been discovered, but none are known for certain to be from *T rex*. Some dinosaurs laid eggs in nests and looked after their young, but again there are no fossils like this for *T rex*.

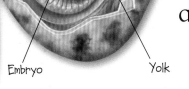

▶ Young *T rex* may have killed small prey such as birds, lizards and newly hatched dinosaurs.

46 It seems that *T rex* grew slowly for about 12–14 years. Then suddenly it grew very fast, putting on about 2 kilograms every day as a teenager. By 20 years it was full-grown.

45 Fossils of individual *T rex* are of different sizes and ages, showing how this dinosaur grew up. Some of the fossil bones are so well preserved that they have 'growth rings' almost like a tree trunk, showing growth speed.

47 Can we tell apart female and male *Tyrannosaurus rex* from their fossils? Some scientists thought that females were bigger, with stronger, thicker bones than the males. However the latest evidence makes this less clear.

▶ In many reptiles today, the adults keep growing with age. However their growth rate gradually reduces, so they get bigger more slowly. It is not certain if dinosaurs such as *T rex* grew like this.

48 The biggest *T rex* found, 'Sue', was about 28 years old when it died. No one knows for certain if *Tyrannosaurus rex* could live longer. As with many of these questions, more fossil finds will help to fill in the details.

Where in the world?

49 T rex was one kind, or species, of dinosaur in a group of species known as the genus *Tyrannosaurus*. Were there any other members of this genus?

50 After T rex fossils were discovered and named over 100 years ago, fossil-hunters began to find the remains of many similar huge predators. Some were given their own names in the genus *Tyrannosaurus*, but most have now been renamed *Tyrannosaurus rex*.

51 *Tarbosaurus*, 'terrifying lizard', was very similar to T rex, almost as big, and it lived at the same time. However its fossils come from Asia – Mongolia and China – rather than North America. Some experts consider it to be another species of *Tyrannosaurus*, called *Tyrannosaurus bataar*. Others think that it's so similar to T rex that it should be called *Tyrannosaurus rex*.

52 Fossils of smaller dinosaurs similar to T rex have been found in Europe. They include 6-metre-long *Eotyrannus*, from more than 100 million years ago, from the Isle of Wight, southern England. Fossils of *Aviatyrannis* from Portugal are even older, from the Jurassic Period.

◄ *Tarbosaurus* had big teeth, tiny arms and many other features similar to T rex. It was named by Russian fossil expert Evgeny Maleev in 1955, exactly 50 years after T rex was named.

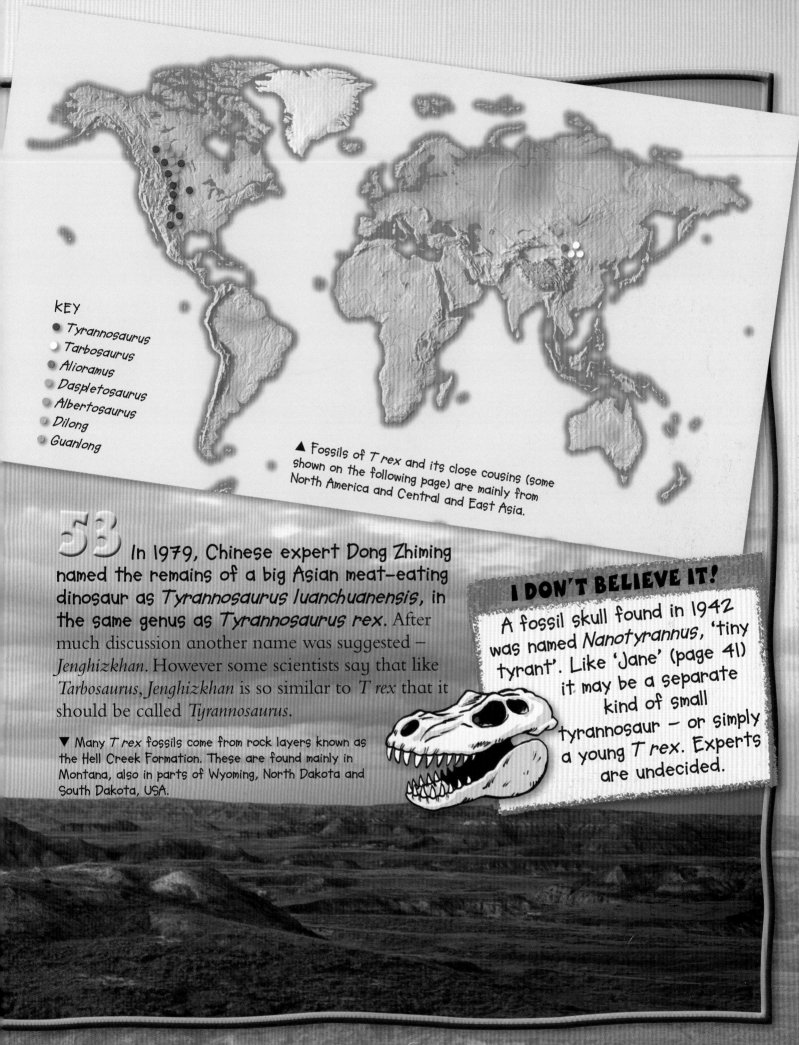

KEY

● Tyrannosaurus
○ Tarbosaurus
● Alioramus
● Daspletosaurus
● Albertosaurus
● Dilong
● Guanlong

▲ Fossils of *T rex* and its close cousins (some shown on the following page) are mainly from North America and Central and East Asia.

53 In 1979, Chinese expert Dong Zhiming named the remains of a big Asian meat-eating dinosaur as *Tyrannosaurus luanchuanensis*, in the same genus as *Tyrannosaurus rex*. After much discussion another name was suggested – *Jenghizkhan*. However some scientists say that like *Tarbosaurus*, *Jenghizkhan* is so similar to *T rex* that it should be called *Tyrannosaurus*.

▼ Many *T rex* fossils come from rock layers known as the Hell Creek Formation. These are found mainly in Montana, also in parts of Wyoming, North Dakota and South Dakota, USA.

I DON'T BELIEVE IT!

A fossil skull found in 1942 was named *Nanotyrannus*, 'tiny tyrant'. Like 'Jane' (page 41) it may be a separate kind of small tyrannosaur – or simply a young *T rex*. Experts are undecided.

Tyrannosaur group

54 **What kind of dinosaur was** *Tyrannosaurus rex?* It belonged to the group called tyrannosaurs, known scientifically as the family *Tyrannosauridae*. These dinosaurs had bones, joints and other features that were different from other predatory dinosaurs. They were part of an even bigger group, the tyrannosauroids.

Tyrannosaurus rex

Nanotyrannus (could be same as Tyrannosaurus)

Tarbosaurus (could be same as Tyrannosaurus)

Tyrannosaurine subfamily

55 One of the first tyrannosauroids was *Guanlong*, 'crown dragon'. Its fossils were discovered in China in 2006 and are about 160 million years old – nearly 100 million years before *Tyrannosaurus rex*. It was 3 metres long and had a strange horn-like plate of bone on its nose.

▲ *Guanlong* may have shown off the crest of thin bone on its head to possible partners at breeding time.

▼ The 'feathers' of *Dilong* were similar to fur and may have kept its body warm.

56 Another early cousin of *T rex* was *Dilong*, 'emperor dragon', also from China. Its fossils date to 130 million years ago. *Dilong* was about 2 metres long when fully grown. It had traces of hair-like feathers on the head and tail. As shown later, some experts suggest *Tyrannosaurus rex* itself may have had some kind of feathers.

Alioramus Daspletosaurus Albertosaurus Gorgosaurus

Other
tyrannosauroids
include:
Alectrosaurus
Appalachiosaurus
Aviatyrannis
Dilong
Dryptosaurus
Eotyrannus
Guanlong
Stokesosaurus

Albertosaurine
subfamily

◄ *T rex* and its main relatives form a group of animals called a family. This was part of a larger group, or superfamily, of big meat eaters.

Tyrannosaurid
family

Tyrannosauroid
superfamily

▼ *Velociraptor* and other raptors were not close cousins of the tyrannosaurs, but members of another meat-eating group, the dromaeosaurs.

Other
meat eaters

Meat eating dinosaurs
or theropods

57 The tyrannosaurs were not the only meat-eating dinosaurs. Others include *Allosaurus*, which was almost as big as *T rex*. It also lived in North America, but 80 million years earlier. *Compsognathus* was a tiny meat eater at just one metre long, and it lived about 150 million years ago. Medium-sized meat eaters called 'raptors' include *Velociraptor* from 75 million years ago and *Deinonychus* dating back 110 million years. Raptors varied in size from about 2–5 metres long. All these meat eaters were in the main dinosaur group called the theropods, or 'bird feet'.

◄ *Compsognathus* chased small prey such as lizards and bugs.

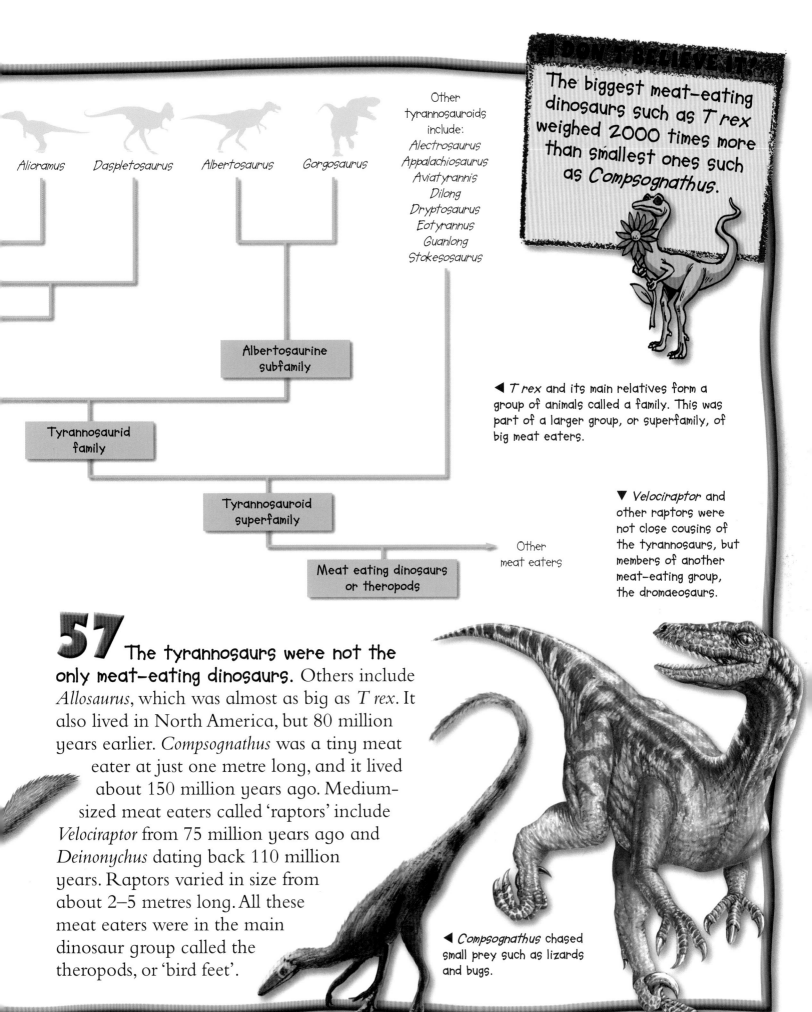

Close cousins

58 In the tyrannosaur group with *T rex* were several of its closest relatives. They were big, fierce dinosaurs, but most lived before *T rex* and were not quite as large.

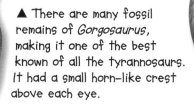

▲ There are many fossil remains of *Gorgosaurus*, making it one of the best known of all the tyrannosaurs. It had a small horn-like crest above each eye.

59 Fossils of *Gorgosaurus*, 'fierce lizard', come mainly from Alberta, Canada and are 75–70 million years old. *Gorgosaurus* was very similar to *Albertosaurus*, although slightly smaller at 8–9 metres long. Like all tyrannosaurs, it had hollow bones and openings in its skull that helped to reduce its weight. Some experts think that *Gorgosaurus* was really a kind of *Albertosaurus* and that its name should be changed.

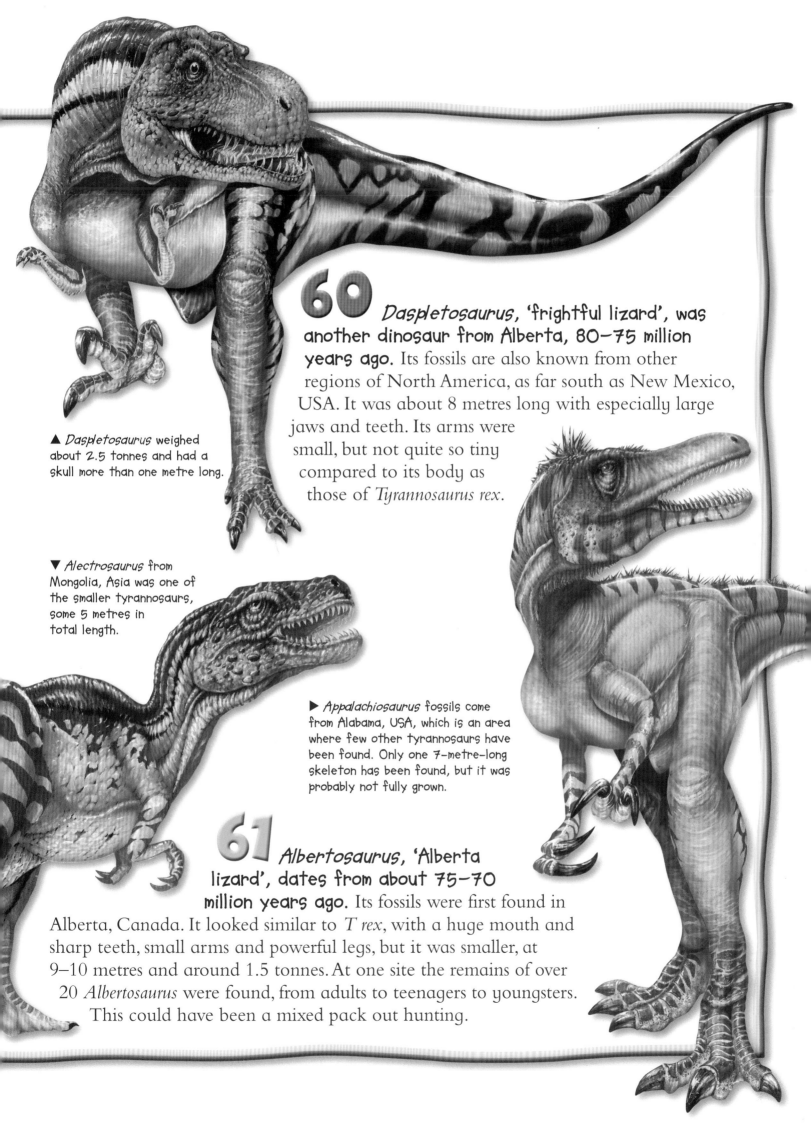

60 *Daspletosaurus*, 'frightful lizard', was another dinosaur from Alberta, 80–75 million years ago. Its fossils are also known from other regions of North America, as far south as New Mexico, USA. It was about 8 metres long with especially large jaws and teeth. Its arms were small, but not quite so tiny compared to its body as those of *Tyrannosaurus rex*.

▲ *Daspletosaurus* weighed about 2.5 tonnes and had a skull more than one metre long.

▼ *Alectrosaurus* from Mongolia, Asia was one of the smaller tyrannosaurs, some 5 metres in total length.

▶ *Appalachiosaurus* fossils come from Alabama, USA, which is an area where few other tyrannosaurs have been found. Only one 7-metre-long skeleton has been found, but it was probably not fully grown.

61 *Albertosaurus*, 'Alberta lizard', dates from about 75–70 million years ago. Its fossils were first found in Alberta, Canada. It looked similar to *T rex*, with a huge mouth and sharp teeth, small arms and powerful legs, but it was smaller, at 9–10 metres and around 1.5 tonnes. At one site the remains of over 20 *Albertosaurus* were found, from adults to teenagers to youngsters. This could have been a mixed pack out hunting.

Discovering T rex

62 The first fossils of T rex were found in the 1870s by Arthur Lakes and John Bell Hatcher, in Wyoming, USA. However these were not recognized as T rex until years later. In 1892, fossil expert Edward Drinker Cope found remains of a big meat eater and named them *Manospondylus*. Over 100 years later these remains were restudied and renamed as T rex.

▲ Edward Drinker Cope (1840–97) named many other kinds of dinosaurs in addition to T rex, including *Camarasaurus*, *Amphicoelias*, *Coelophysis*, *Hadrosaurus* and *Monoclonius*.

▶ The fossil bones of big dinosaurs such as T rex are solid stone and very heavy. Many years ago, horses dragged them from rocky, remote areas to the nearest road or railway.

63 In 1900, again in Wyoming, leading fossil collector Barnum Brown found the first partial skeleton of *Tyrannosaurus rex*, rather than scattered single bones and teeth. At first the fossils were named as *Dynamosaurus* by Henry Fairfield Osborn of the American Museum of Natural History in New York.

66 *T rex* fossils have always been greatly prized by museums, exhibitions and private collectors. In 1941, the fossils that Brown found in 1902 were sold to the Carnegie Museum of Natural History in Pittsburgh, Pennsylvania, for a huge sum of money. Searching for, selling and buying *T rex* fossils continues today.

▼ Barnum Brown was the most famous fossil-hunter of his time. He sometimes wore a thick fur coat — even when digging for fossils in the scorching sun.

64 Barnum Brown discovered parts of another *Tyrannosaurus rex* fossil skeleton at Hell Creek, Montana, in 1902. In 1905, Osborn wrote a scientific description of these remains and called them *Tyrannosaurus rex*. This was the first time the official name was used. In a way, it was when *T rex* was 'born'.

BARNUM BROWN — DINOSAUR DETECTIVE

Barnum Brown (1873-1963) collected not only dinosaur fossils, but fossils of all kinds, and other scientific treasures such as crystals. He and his teams worked for the American Museum of Natural History in New York. They travelled to remote places, and if there were rivers but no roads, they used a large raft as a floating base camp. They worked fast too, often blasting apart rocks with dynamite. Brown also made a living by informing oil companies about the best places to drill for oil.

65 In 1906, Brown found an even better part-skeleton of *Tyrannosaurus rex* in Montana. The same year, Osborn realized that the *Dynamosaurus* fossils were extremely similar to *Tyrannosaurus rex*, so he renamed those too as *Tyrannosaurus rex*. The public began to hear about this huge, fierce, meat-eating monster from long ago, and soon its fame was growing fast.

Working with fossils

▼ There are several stages to the fossilization process, which can take many millions of years.

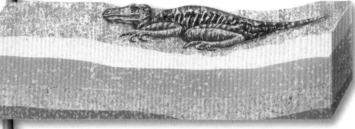

1. A dinosaur dies and falls into a lake or river, where it sinks to the bottom. The flesh and other soft body parts rot away or are eaten by water-dwelling creatures.

2. The bones and teeth are buried under layers of mud and sand. Silica and other minerals from the rock seep into the bones, filling any available gaps.

3. Over a period of millions of years, minerals replace the original dinosaur bones entirely, but preserve their shape and form. The bones have become fossils.

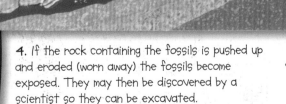

4. If the rock containing the fossils is pushed up and eroded (worn away) the fossils become exposed. They may then be discovered by a scientist so they can be excavated.

67 Like all animal fossils, those of *T rex* are of the harder parts of the body. They have been preserved in rocks and, over many millions of years, gradually turned to stone.

68 For dinosaurs, the body parts that form fossils are mainly bones, teeth, claws, horns, and less often, skin. There are also fossilized eggs, footprints or trackways, coprolites (droppings) and other clues.

69 Like many other prehistoric creatures, most *T rex* fossils are broken scraps, squashed bits and crushed pieces. They are often very difficult to put together, and scientists have trouble identifying the original animals.

I DON'T BELIEVE IT!

Some *T rex* fossils show injuries that may have been caused by the teeth of other *T rex*. Perhaps they were fighting over food, territory, or breeding partners, or who was boss.

▶ *Archaeopteryx*, the earliest known bird, lived about 80 million years before *T rex*. Its bones show many similarities to small meat-eating dinosaurs.

70 Reptiles today are cold-blooded, but were *T rex* and some other dinosaurs warm-blooded, like mammals and birds? Fossils show that *T rex*'s bone structure and growth rate were similar to mammals and birds. There is also evidence that the chemical make-up of its preserved bones resembles birds. But there is no complete proof one way or the other.

▶ A palaeontologist working at a *T rex* dig site. A variety of tools and special equipment is needed to help remove the fossils from the ground.

71 In 2008, 68-million-year-old fossils of *T rex* (named 'B rex' by palaeontologists) were unearthed in Montana, USA. Examining these very well-preserved bones with a microscope showed they were similar to those of living female birds. So 'B rex' may well have been a female *T rex* producing eggs inside her body when she died aged 15–20 years.

Rebuilding T rex

72 Fossil experts use preserved bones and other parts of T rex to show what it looked like when alive. The bones are also compared to those of similar animals alive today, known as comparative anatomy. For T rex, similar living animals include crocodiles, lizards – and birds.

73 Some fossil bones have patches, grooves and ridges called 'muscle scars'. They show where the animal's muscles were joined to the bones in life. This helps experts to work out how the muscles pulled the bones and how T rex moved when it was alive.

74 As with other extinct creatures, there are no remains of T rex's soft body parts such as the stomach, guts, heart and lungs. These were eaten by scavengers soon after death or were rotted away. However experts can use comparative anatomy with living creatures to imagine what T rex's soft body parts looked like.

▼ Fossil dinosaur skin has a scaly surface, similar to many of today's reptiles.

75 Skin and scales of dinosaurs sometimes form fossils. However they are the colour of the rocks that make the fossils, not the colour of the original skin and scales. So we have no way of knowing T rex's true colour in life.

◄ Close cousins of T rex have been preserved with simple hair–like feathers on their skin. It may be possible that T rex also had feathers.

▲ This reconstruction of *T rex* shows the modern idea of its body position, with tail held straight out behind. When the skull is moved from the trolley to the front end of the neck bones, it will be positioned low, not high as previously thought.

▶ For many years, *T rex* was thought to hold its head up high and drag its tail along the ground.

76 The first reconstructions of *T rex* showed it standing almost upright like a kangaroo. However from its bone and joint shapes, most experts now think that it held its head and body level with the ground, balanced over its big back legs by its long, heavy tail.

The story of Sue

77 The biggest *Tyrannosaurus rex* found so far is 'Sue'. Its official code number is FMNH PR2081, from the Field Museum of Natural History in Chicago, USA.

78 'Sue' is named after its discoverer, Sue Hendrickson. She was working at a fossil dig in 1990 near the town of Faith, in South Dakota, USA, when she uncovered parts of a massive *T rex*. An entire team of people helped to dig up and clean the remains.

79 'Sue' is amazingly complete for a fossil animal, with about four-fifths of its teeth, bones and other parts preserved. The dinosaur was probably covered with mud soon after it died, which prevented scavenging animals from cracking open or carrying away its bones.

80 'Sue' dates from between 67 and 65.5 million years ago. It measures 12.8 metres from nose to tail-tip and 4 metres tall at the hips. The weight of 'Sue' when alive was probably between 5.5 and 6.5 tonnes.

◄ Sue Hendrickson with the fossil foot of 'Sue'. As well as finding 'Sue' the *T rex*, Sue Hendrickson is an expert diver and has explored shipwrecks and sunken cities.

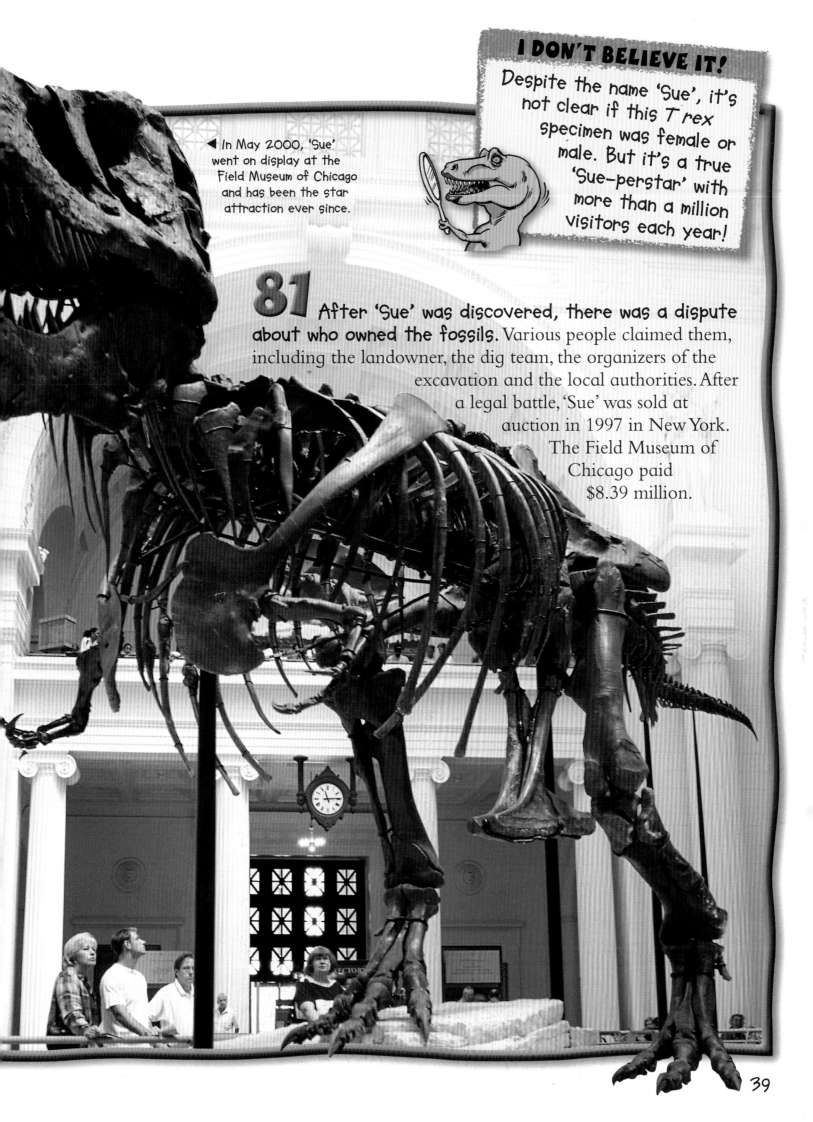

◀ In May 2000, 'Sue' went on display at the Field Museum of Chicago and has been the star attraction ever since.

81 **After 'Sue' was discovered, there was a dispute about who owned the fossils.** Various people claimed them, including the landowner, the dig team, the organizers of the excavation and the local authorities. After a legal battle, 'Sue' was sold at auction in 1997 in New York. The Field Museum of Chicago paid $8.39 million.

Stan, Jane and the rest

82 Apart from 'Sue', there are more than 30 other sets of *T rex* fossils. Some are just a few bones and teeth, while others are well preserved, fairly complete skeletons.

83 'Stan' is named after its discoverer Stan Sacrisen. Code numbered BHI 3033, it was dug up near Buffalo, South Dakota, USA in 1992 by a team from the Black Hills Institute. 'Stan' was about 12.2 metres long and 3 tonnes in weight, with 199 bones and 58 teeth. Some bones show signs of injuries that had healed, including broken ribs, a damaged neck and a tooth wound in the skull.

▶ 'Stan' is now at the Black Hills Museum in Hill City, South Dakota.

84 'Wankel rex', specimen MOR 555, was found by Kathy Wankel in 1988. It was excavated by a team from the Museum of the Rockies and is now on show at that museum in Bozeman, Montana.

85 'Tinker', also called 'Kid Rex', was a young *Tyrannosaurus rex*. About two-thirds adult size, it was found in 1998 in South Dakota and named after the leader of the fossil-hunting team, Ron 'Tinker' Frithiof.

86 'Jane' is specimen BMRP 2002.4.1 at the Burpee Museum of Natural History, Rockford, Illinois, USA. Found in Montana, it's smaller than a full grown *Tyrannosaurus rex*, at 6.5 metres long and 650–700 kilograms. Some experts believe it is a part-grown youngster, probably 10–12 years old when it died. Others say it is a similar but smaller kind of dinosaur named *Nanotyrannus*.

▶ The fossils of 'Jane' from Montana's Hell Creek took more than four years to dig out, clean up and put together for display.

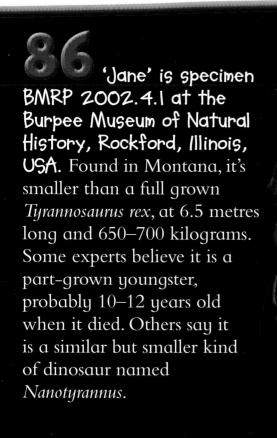

A new name for T rex

You will need:
pictures of *T rex* in different poses
pen   paper

Copy some pictures of *T rex* onto your paper. Imagine you and your friends have discovered their fossils and given them nicknames. Write these next to your drawings. Perhaps *T rex* should be named after you?

41

Bigger than the 'king'

87 Until the 1990s, *Tyrannosaurus rex* was famous as the biggest predatory land creature of all time. But the past few years have seen discoveries of even bigger meat-eating or carnivorous dinosaurs.

88 Fossils of *Giganotosaurus*, 'southern giant reptile', were uncovered in 1993 in Patagonia, Argentina. This huge hunter was slightly bigger than *T rex*, at more than 13 metres long and weighing over 6 tonnes. *Giganotosaurus* lived earlier than *T rex*, about 95–90 million years ago.

89 Fossils of *Spinosaurus* were first found in Egypt in 1912. This predator lived 100–95 million years ago, and had long, bony rods sticking up from its back that may have held up a 'sail' of skin. The original remains suggested a big predator, but not as big as *T rex*. However recent finds indicate that *Spinosaurus* may have been larger, maybe 16 metres long and 7 tonnes in weight.

QUIZ

Put these dinosaurs in order of size, biggest to smallest:
Tyrannosaurus rex Deinonychus
Brachiosaurus Spinosaurus
Compsognathus Giganotosaurus

Answers:
Brachiosaurus, Spinosaurus, Giganotosaurus, Tyrannosaurus rex, Deinonychus, Compsognathus

90 *Carcharodontosaurus*, 'shark tooth lizard', was another massive hunter from North Africa. It was first named in 1931 and lived 100–95 million years ago. Recent discoveries in Morocco and Niger show that it could have been about the same size as *T rex*.

91 Another *T rex*-sized dinosaur was *Mapusaurus*, which lived in Argentina around the same time as *T rex* lived in North America. It was not as heavily built as *T rex*, weighing about 3 tonnes.

▼ This skull of *Carcharodontosaurus* measures more than 1.7 metres in length, with teeth 20 centimetres long. The human skull just in front of it gives an idea of just how big this dinosaur was.

► *T rex* and the other meat eaters were not the biggest dinosaurs by far. Much larger are huge plant eaters such as *Brachiosaurus* and *Argentinosaurus*.

T rex superstar

92 *Tyrannosaurus rex* is far more than a big meat-eating dinosaur. It's a world superstar, alongside such famous creatures as the great white shark, blue whale, gorilla, tiger and golden eagle. If *Tyrannosaurus rex* was alive today and could charge money for using its name, pictures, sponsorships and advertising, it would be mega-rich!

93 Ever since its fossils were discovered, *T rex* has starred in books, plays and movies. It's featured in films such as *The Lost World* (first made in 1925, then again in 1960 and 1992), several *King Kong* movies, the animated *The Land Before Time* (1988), and the *Night at the Museum* movies (2006, 2009).

▼ In *Night at the Museum*, Rexy the *T rex* skeleton looks fierce but is really quite cute and chases bones like a puppy.

I DON'T BELIEVE IT!

T rex was one of the stars of the *Jurassic Park* movies. However it didn't live in the Jurassic Period, it lived 80 million years later at the end of the Cretaceous Period.

▶ In *T rex: Back to the Cretaceous* (1998), Ally finds a mysterious egg-like rock — which transports her back to the end of the Dinosaur Age.

94 In movies, *Tyrannosaurus rex* is perhaps most famous from the *Jurassic Park* series. These began with *Jurassic Park* itself in 1993, then *The Lost World: Jurassic Park* in 1997, and *Jurassic Park 3* in 2001. *Tyrannosaurus rex is* shown breaking out of its fenced enclosure, attacking people and generally causing havoc — but also looking after and protecting its baby with great care.

95 *Toy Story* movies, games and other products feature an unusual *Tyrannosaurus rex* toy called 'Rex' who is nervous, weedy and worried. This is very unlike the usual fearsome character given to *T rex*.

▶ The *T rex* of *Jurassic Park* tries to sniff out human prey, but in the end it saves them from being attacked by marauding raptor dinosaurs.

What next for T rex?

96 Why did *T rex* die out 65 million years ago, along with all other dinosaurs? The main suggestion is that a huge lump of rock from space, an asteroid, hit Earth and caused worldwide disasters of giant waves, volcanic eruptions and a dust cloud that blotted out the Sun. In this end-of Cretaceous mass extinction no dinosaurs, not even the great *T rex*, could survive.

▶ A dinosaur fan comes face to face with *T rex* at the *Walking with Dinosaurs* tour, 2009. Animatronic (mechanical model) dinosaurs move and roar, but unlike the real ones, they are harmless.

97 Our ideas about *T rex* do not stand still. As scientists discover more fossils and invent new methods of studying them, we learn more about *T rex* and the other animals and plants of its time.

98 Could *Tyrannosaurus rex* or similar dinosaurs still survive today, in thick jungle or on remote mountains? Most of the world's land has now been explored or photographed from aircraft and satellites. Sadly, there's no sign of *T rex* or other big unknown animals.

99 Could *T rex* somehow be brought back to life from its fossil remains? Even with the latest scientific methods, this is still a very remote and faraway possibility. Even if it worked, where would *Tyrannosaurus rex* live and what would it eat? Its habitat, with the climate, scenery, plants and animals, is long gone.

100 *Tyrannosaurus rex* no longer holds the record as the biggest land predator of all time. But it's such a well known celebrity around the world that it will probably remain the most famous dinosaur, and one of the most popular creatures of all, for many years to come.

Index

Entries in **bold** refer to main subject entries. Entries in *italics* refer to illustrations.